WILLIAM PLOMER

WILLIAM PLOMER

Selected Poems
edited by Neilson MacKay

LITTLE ISLAND PRESS

Lodgemore Lane,
Stroud, GL5 3EQ

Published in the United Kingdom by
Little Island Press, Stroud

Introductory and editorial material
© Neilson MacKay 2016

Poems © Estate of William Plomer

Image on p.6: 'William Plomer, 1952'
by Bill Brandt © Bill Brandt Archive

First Published 2016

ISBN 978–0–9935056–3–8

Series design by t.r.u
typographic research unit

Typeset in Bembo MT

CONTENTS

Said William Plomer to his barber: 'A little more off the
back, please.' 'That's right, sir,' came the reply. 'It wouldn't
do to have you looking like a poet.' Apocryphal? Possibly.
Yet such drollery has the ring of prophecy. In a letter to
John Lehmann in 1931 Plomer confessed, waggishly, that
he had 'never pretended to be a poet', not even to himself.
Ted Walker (who did look like a poet) observed that
Plomer's demeanour suggested not so much a writer as
a magnanimous doctor. Walker was late to the party. As
Plomer recalled it: 'I have actually been congratulated [by
a stranger] on my successful treatment of a difficult case of
hydrocele' (*the accumulation of serous fluid in the testes*). Farce
followed him like a guided missile.

'Plomer, is emphatically of the minority, i.e. of the
section of writers, the real intelligentsia, the unconventional,
critical-minded literary artists whom the British public
in general don't *like*, and therefore only buy in restricted
quantities.' That was Edward Garnett in 1935. In 1972
several newspapers had tipped him, like a horse, as the next
Poet Laureate, a role Cecil Day-Lewis famously compared
to being 'put out to grass'. To Plomer's relief, the post went
to John Betjeman, who hated the job so much he considered
resigning. The timing, in any event, was off: Plomer died in
1973, just three days before the publication of *The Butterfly
Ball and the Grasshopper's Feast*, a cheerful, Whitbread-
winning exercise in whimsy which cruelly outstripped
sales of his *Collected Poems* (also published in 1973) – the
book upon which his poetic reputation mostly rests. At the
time, Plomer looked ripe for canonisation. His friends were
the right ones: Leonard and Virginia Woolf, T.S. Eliot,
E.M Forster, W.H. Auden, Christopher Isherwood,

J.R. Ackerley, Day-Lewis, Stephen Spender, Edmund Blunden, the Sitwells. Today he is largely forgotten.

A shame. His poems are a thing apart, or rather, a continent apart: Plomer shares – *should* share – with his once friend and collaborator Roy Campbell the plaudit 'best South African poet'. Campbell, by all accounts, is more fun to remember (Plomer never suspended his wife from a balcony, not least because he never married), but his fire-in-the-belly pentameters look ill at ease against Plomer's natural and shifting rhythms, his awkward, cool repose. Plomer 'had the singular gift', said Laurens van der Post, 'of being angry in a classical sense ... a vision that does not blur, but makes the vision clearer'. Angry? Maybe. Classical? Yes – the poems are scrupulously crafted, delimited, self-effacing. In 'They' he writes:

It's plain that by deviating in your own way
you've made what you have. You've made it
clear, durable, pointed as a cluster of crystals.

Durability, visual accuracy, rigorous economy of language – such were Plomer's main-line faculties.

A consummate all-rounder, Plomer, in a career spanning five decades, produced ten books of poetry, five novels (several popular successes), five volumes of short stories, two biographies (*Cecil Rhodes* and *Ali Pasha*), four librettos (for Benjamin Britten), scores of essays, articles and reviews (for *The Spectator*, *The Nation*, *The Criterion* and others), and three edited diaries (*Kilvert's Diary* is the best known). He was co-editor, with Campbell, of *Voorslag*, a literary review founded to counteract the chilling effects of proto-apartheid legislation in South Africa, featuring writing in both English and Afrikaans. In later life he was a publisher's reader and literary advisor for Jonathan Cape, where he was an early and ebullient proponent of Ted Hughes, Arthur Koestler, Stevie Smith, John Betjeman, John Fowles, Vladimir Nabokov, Alan Paton and Ian Fleming. (No Plomer, no Bond.) From 1937–51 he broadcast intermittently with the BBC a number of lit-programmes, including *The Critics*, on which he discussed new books with the novelist Rose Macaulay. He was awarded the Queen's Medal for Poetry in 1963 and a CBE in 1965.

Looking over this litany of achievements, one can't help but wonder if he spread himself too thin. Was he a poet who was also a novelist, or a novelist who was also a poet? Take your pick. Either way, Plomer's knack for working across generic boundaries has made him difficult to place. Such divided loyalties find their correlative in his near-frenetic preoccupation with his own situatedness: England, South Africa – he identified with both but belonged to neither: 'Since nobody,' he wrote in his autobiography, 'if a cat happens to have kittens in an oven, regards them as biscuits, I should be no more justified in pretending to be a South African than declaring myself a Bantu.' By the age of 28, Plomer had been variously 'a trader in Zululand, an apprentice farmer in the (rugged) mountains on the Basutoland border, unemployed in Japan, a tourist in Russia and an alleged Λόρδος [Lord] in Greece'. The poems, not by chance, are correspondingly peripatetic: Africa, Japan, Greece, England, they are of – *in* – such places. ('Read Plomer,' goes the caption attached to his caricature in *Punch*, 'if you'd like a tip on / Africa, London, or the land of Nippon.') Looking back, he felt he had something in common with the aloof, nomadic Axel Heyst, from Conrad's *Victory*. He learned much, too, from Eliot:

                              My need
As a poet (not every poet's) is this –
To be immersed in a neutral solution, which
Alone provides an interim, until through the grey
Expectant film invisible writing comes clean.

No identity can be a desirable thing:
To have a face with features noticed less
Than one's range of expression, so that photographed
It never looks twice the same, and people say
'But that's not you!'

'Inert, neutral, unchanged', Plomer might have been the
platinum in Eliot's chemical analogy, though his escape
from personality was an actual success (most 'impersonal'
poets usually turn out to be as candid as everyone else). The
poems are not, as are, say, Robert Lowell's, an arena for
'working out' his jumble of dualities; if he assumes a mask,
it is to hide his face. The lyric 'I', when present, is voided of
its interiority. He won't let us know him. He is not sure he
knows himself.

In his life of Forster, P.N. Furbank attested to the split in
Plomer between irony and feeling: one part sentiment, one
part 'foxy aplomb'. That's one way of saying he had a funny
side. As a light verse writer, Martin Seymour-Smith wrote,
'there is no one like him in the world'. Plomer's peculiar
brand of puckish wit, his obstinate penchant for detective-
story macabre, found its natural outlet in balladry. Not
included in this selection, the ballads nonetheless deserve
a mention – they are, alas, 'his most celebrated poems', as
Phillip Larkin noted. Compared to his more serious work
(though light verse can, of course, be serious), the ballads, it
seems to me, have dated. Still, his gallery of nasties is hard to

resist: the woman who happily agrees to her own murder; the former Dean of Westminster who inadvertently swallows the fossilised heart of Louis Quatortze at a dinner party; the couple whose open-house is cut short by the discovery in a cupboard of 'the severed thigh of a plump brunette'; the housekeeper who goes missing picking mushrooms and subsequently dies – the more heartless, that last one, as it arises from a true story. Such performance-ready silliness would crack a smile on even the stoniest of faces, though censure replaced the smile for some: 'I have once or twice been reproached for cruelty and a choice of sordid themes,' wrote Plomer, adding, 'no defence seems necessary.' The poems' unpleasantness was merely reflective of an age 'for which unpleasant would be a very mild term'.

★ ★ ★

William Charles Franklyn Plomer – the surname rhymes with 'bloomer' – was born on 10 December 1903, in Pietersburg (now Polokwane), South Africa, of English parents. His father was an itinerant magistrate. In 1905 the family moved to Louis Trichardt, Limpopo. Times were tough. The township was largely abandoned and malaria rife – 'romantic,' Plomer wrote, 'in a Rider Haggardish way' (Haggard would have enjoyed that 'ish'). His younger brother contracted malaria and died, after which Plomer was sent to England, a country he recognised, he wrote, 'as a mirror recognises a face'. He was educated at Beechmont, Kent, which he loathed, and later at Rugby. He cut his teeth on Chaucer, Eliot, Dostoevsky and D.H. Lawrence.

Fearing that Oxford might make him 'more of a pedant and a prig than I am', Plomer returned to South Africa and took work as an apprentice sheep farmer in Molteno, Cape

Province ('A Basuto Coming of Age') where he composed his first poems. These first offerings were exiguous and wanting, bumptious and sentimental, all gloss ('O aqueous evening skies / pavilioning the world with silken light, / you rest'). He sent the lot to Harold Monro at the Poetry Bookshop in London, with an accompanying letter that no doubt made Monro smile: 'I am familiar with all the "moderns", except John Drinkwater, A.E. Housman, and a good many very minor people. Is it necessary for me to read J.D., A.E.H., and the v. minor people?' Monro replied benevolently. A better poem followed:

I came upon the poplars as the sun goes down.
Staccato, as the sun departs,
The sharp dark trees
Pierce the stark earth like darts.

In 1922 Plomer opened a trading post with his father in Entumeni, Zululand, where he cultivated an interest in the Zulus and their language. He was attracted first to their bodies: 'the young bucks, descendants of Chaka's braves' – reminiscent of Melville's comparison of the Marquesans with the peoples of New York – aroused him. Eros gave way to agape. The racialised complex of South African society, virulent and epidemic, prevented any but furtive intimacies. 'It occurred to me quite early in life,' Plomer recalls, 'that the terms "black" and "white" were too arbitrary. One thing was rigidly clear – that the presumed line between so-called white and so-called black must never be crossed – at least openly.'

His first novel, *Turbott Wolfe*, was published by Leonard and Virginia Woolf at the Hogarth Press in 1926, followed by *Notes for Poems*, his first book of poetry, in 1927. The novel, which featured as its eponymous hero an English negrophile who encourages miscegenation, sparked outrage. A review in *The Natal Advertiser* carried the title 'A Nasty Book on a Nasty Subject', expressing lament at the passing of the great days of 'Fitzpatrick's "Jock of the Bushveld", or Rider Haggard's vivid and inspiring romances in which white men were white and the kafir was black, but a gentleman'. Astringent, unsparing in its assault on white South Africa's 'insular complacency', Plomer called it 'a violent ejaculation, a protest, a nightmare, a phantasmagoria'. Richard Church called it a work of genius; *South African Nation* called it pornography. Aged 23 and already courting opprobrium, Roy Campbell wrote of him in *The Wayzgoose*:

Plomer, 'twas you who, though a boy in age,
Awoke a sleepy continent to rage,
Who dared alone to thrash a craven race
And hold a mirror to its dirty face.

Plomer is 'interested in technique in the right way', F.R. Leavis noted, 'For he is interested primarily in the world he lives in, and technique for him is the problem of getting the "feel" of living into verse.' But what is that 'feel?' It is a poetry of place, of places. It is topographical – geophysical. Plomer shares Auden's fondness for geology – for petrology, in particular. If Auden found in limestone an honesty (limestone is, as Auden said of his own face, fault-ridden), Plomer's quarry yields tougher things:

In the wild fig trees,
Whose sinews are moulded
To the curves of the stone,
And whose roots are thrust
In a crevice of dust,

13

Clinging tightly within
To the veins of the quartz,
And fed on the secret
And tasting of stone.

Plomer is not *difficult*. He has in common with The
Movement (the exponents of which he predates) an
impatience for opacity. In the best poems, form and content
are blended, their interdependence discernible to the most
general of general readers. In their directness of address –
though not, it bears mentioning, in their stylistic import
– the poems lean closer to the linguistic compressions of
Hardy, Thomas and the Georgians than to the oblique
bookishness of the high moderns. A self-described 'lone
prospector', his 'gain' – sometimes rubble, sometimes 'a
handful of semi-precious stones' – was, though inconsistent,
sui generis.

If Plomer lacks the 'overmastering' vision of an Eliot
or Yeats, as one critic put it, this is because he does: 'My
own predilections in poetry,' he wrote to Spender, 'are
for the sensory, pictorial and plastic rather than for the
philosophical, metaphysical or political.'

Plomer's 'African phase' – really an Anglophone
modernist phase played out in African contexts – is a love
letter to stuff: animal stuff, vegetable stuff, mineral stuff.
Matter abounds: dry stalks, small roots, loxias, spacious
upland kraals. Throw in a handful of Africanisms – jackals,
cicadas, giraffes, zebus, antelopes – and you've got the
measure of 'Namaqualand After Rain', 'Ula Masondo's
Dream' and a clutch of others. In 'The Ruined Farm' and
others, the tendency is towards a kind of imagism:

A peaceful, archangelic sun
Sank low, grew larger to the sight,
And drew across each huge ravine
The huger curtains of the night;

Silence within the roofless house
Undid her hair and shook it free,
The footpad jackal passed her there,
And bats flew round the cactus tree.

A pleasant, nursery rhyme-ish scene that might have
tickled T.E. Hulme. The effect is glacial, non-committed,
immediate, set in the terrain of the perpetual present. Silence,
personified, seems benign enough. Something changes:

Each quiet afternoon was bitter,
Was overcharged with warning,
And Silence waited where the snake lay coiled
And mocked at each mild, bright morning.

Plomer's landscapes ('filled / With heaped-up silence rift
and rut') are fraught, brimming with just-around-the-
corner crises. In the best poems, imagism is sacrificed on the
altar of last minute symbolic abstraction. In 'The Scorpion',
the best of these best, the flooded Limpopo and Tugela
wash up, among other detritus ('Melons, maize, domestic
thatch'), the body of a black woman 'bruised / By rocks,
and rolling on the shore'. Discrete particulars ('lolling
breasts', 'bleeding eyes', 'beads and bells') are in the final
stanza transfigured:

That was the Africa we knew,
Where, wandering alone,

15

We saw, heraldic in the heat,
A scorpion on a stone.

Once a life, now flotsam. Plomer's 'natives' are part and parcel of the cruel land they inhabit – itself an extended metaphor for the cruel indifference with which they are treated by the metropole. That concern for people, for any life but his own, was a constant. The reflection in a Tugela pool of a young Zulu 'Who on a concertina improvised / A slow recurrent tune, subdued / By want of hope' gains its poignancy in the later fact of his death, 'while ... new cars / Hissed past like rockets / Loaded with white men hurrying like mad'. The pathos is palpable.

When *Voorslag* went south in 1926, Plomer went east, to Japan, where he lived for three years (he had only planned to stay a fortnight). The morning after his arrival the headlines read: 'DESCENDANT OF SHAKESPEARE ARRIVES IN JAPAN!' En route, Plomer had let slip that the name of his maternal great-grandmother was Mary Arden, doubtless laying the Shakespeare connection on thick, and the Japanese got the wrong end of the stick. He secured a teaching post, with the help of Edmund Blunden – then visiting professor of English at the Imperial University, Tokyo – read widely, entered into a relationship with a Japanese man, and gradually 'Japanezed' himself. His verse, too, took on something of the still-life, syllabic tautness that is unique to Japanese poetry, probing the delicate balance between '*morae*' (syllables) and '*ku*' (phrases), without quite yielding to the period or post-period verse forms (haiku, waka, etc.) that are peculiarly Japanese as such. The poems are knowingly artificial, slight, stilted, colourful but curiously plastic, ranging from the alliterative, Stevensian fun of 'Hotel Magnificent' to the ersatz imagism of 'The Gingko

Tree'. The latter's pentasyllabic prettiness is wittingly false, like paper flowers left by a roadside accident:

Chrome-yellow in the blue,
   Tremolando tree,
Flute-like aquarelle,
   Pure fragility.

The growing threat of Japanese nationalism, culminating in 1928 with the establishment of the poorly named Peace Preservation Department, unnerved him. He had, in any case, outstayed his welcome. In March 1929 he travelled 'home' by way of the Trans-Siberian Railway, which took him through a country in which 'he had often lived and suffered vicariously' via Tolstoy, Dostoevsky, Turgenev, Gorki, Gogol and Burkin. He arrived in London to the open arms of Bloomsbury – then on the wane – and its reigning monarchs, Leonard and Virginia Woolf. Woolf (Virginia), perspicacious to the letter, described Plomer as 'A compressed inarticulate young man, thickly coated with a universal manner … tells a nice dry prim story; but has the wild eyes which I once noted in Tom [Eliot], & take to be the true index of what goes on within.' His 'mask' was beginning to slip.

In May 1930 Plomer set off with his friend – the painter, Anthony Butts – to Athens. 'I can't tell you how much I like this country,' he wrote Spender in July 1930, 'The sun always shines. There are more men than women.' A rush of sensuous experience followed. He fell in love, somewhat predictably, with a sailor, the subject of 'Three Pinks': a Cavafy-esque, erotically charged love lyric. 'Lotus-eating' – swimming off the bays of Glyphada or Vouliagmeni, dining late out of doors at Psychiko, mornings alone at the Zappeion Gardens – did not keep him from his work. He read voraciously, corresponded with Cavafy, to whom he had been introduced by Forster, and composed some of his finest poems. 'Corfu' is one:

Across the old fortezza fall
The crystal rulings of the rain,
The moon above Albania burns
Fitful as a brigand's dire,
And no boat passes out to sea.

This poem, 'Still Life' and 'The Ruins' impressed Eliot, who published all three in *The Criterion* between 1930 and 1931. Quietly sensuous, tranquil, near-symbolic and vivid, these 'Phillelenisms', as Plomer grouped them, are moments of aesthetic arrival. But they are also, at kernel, tourist poems – the product, much like the rest of his work to this point, of what Plomer described as 'a series of disjointed contacts with different worlds, like scenes from different plays made to succeed one another but not composing a single play'.

It was not until he returned to England that Plomer began to reap the rewards of a fixed environment. He moved first to Lingen, Herefordshire, and completed his first batch of memoirs, *Double Lives* (published later in 1943). Then to London, publishing his second book of poetry, *The Fivefold Screen* (1932), and two novels, *Sado* (1931) and *The Case is Altered* (1932), a best-seller. He left Hogarth, amicably, in 1933. He took work as a publisher's reader for Cape in 1937. At first blush, the 'English' poems are little *about* England, but we are simply in familiar territory; the threat, by then the reality, of war, underpins 'September Evening', 'A Walk in Würzburg' and 'A Charm Against Trouble' (Plomer's 'profoundest utterance', according to Forster). Before long his attention turned, once again, to

South Africa. In 'The Shortest Day', a profoundly moving, rhythmically narcotic elegy (and to my mind one of his best poems) the speaker, enjoying 'fine food and room-warmed wine', turns his gaze outward to the 'white, quiet, boatless, motorless, / Shortest-day sea' and thinks of the slave ships and the lost souls off the Cape of Good Hope:

For some there is no sedation, not in a high warm room
Above the December sea; in company, they are apart,
And homeless at home; and love, of which they hear much,
Is a distant light. Facing the sea now, he
Dreams of the drowned.

In the 1940s and '50s Plomer's poetic output grew fallow. A crop of ballads, *The Dorking Thigh and Other Satires*, appeared in 1945, and another, *A Shot in the Park* (published in the US as *Borderline Ballads*), in 1955, followed five years later by the first edition of his *Collected Poems*. Between 1951 and 1968 he collaborated with Benjamin Britten on four operas: *Gloriana* (1953), *Curlew River* (1964), *The Burning Fiery Furnace* (1966) and *The Prodigal Son* (1968). In 1966 he published *Taste and Remember*, his seventh book of verse, with Cape, to wide acclaim. 'Your hand, ear and eye are now so sure and exact,' Rupert Hart-Davis wrote to him. It was followed, in 1972, by *Celebrations*, his final work. The late poems are, in batches, about poetry – or rather, about Plomer's poetry. Self-conscious though curiously reconciled, they betray a formal and thematic confidence lacking in his earlier work. Some are explanatory – vindicatory, even – of his early offerings. In 'They' ('they' being Plomer's critics), the prevailing, bitter message is 'take it or leave it':

Oddly supposing some judgment needed from them
yet always flummoxed by the imaginative,
or prophetic, or creatively marginal,
they compare it to what they fall for –
the trivial, the trendy, the ephemeral.

In 'Now', a deeply sad, deeply humane poem, a widow is
forced to sell her house and its accompanying knick-knacks
('rare and hand-made undiscovered things are waiting
/ finely made to last, things handed down). Sadder still,
the woman is Plomer, her knick-knacks his poems; there
comes near the middle an apologia for his refusal to join the
modernist phalanx:

Prodding and peeping in this acre of jungle,
once a garden, a modernizer
may break his leg, snared
by a rusty croquet-hoop
or the lead rim of a half buried
ornamental cistern.
There's no gardener now.

At the poem's close, Plomer ends with the hope:

that these few pretty things
inherited or acquired, outlasting me
may be cherished for what they are
more than for what they'd fetch:
Who, you may ask, is to inherit them?
Leaving the world, I leave them to the world.'

He died in Lewes, East Sussex, in 1973.

Whither Plomer then? Of his twenty-eight books, just two are in print (*Turbott Wolfe* and *Kilvert's Diary*). A selected poems appeared in 1985, homing in on the African poems, and a biography, by Peter F. Alexander, in 1990. Back then, Alexander forecast that Plomer would 'shake off obscurity rapidly', patently jumping the gun. (At this distance of time, we can, perhaps, let go of our hats.) In a review of that book, John Bayley noted that the 'academic perpetuity' accorded Yeats and Eliot, who go marching on whatever the weather, does not extend to the writers who give the period 'its actual and particular flavour': Cyril Connoly, Arthur Koestler, Stephen Spender, Alun Lewis, Peter Quennell, Dylan Thomas, William Plomer. Of these, Plomer – with the possible exception of Quennell – has fallen furthest.

There are reasons. In 1943, Denyls Val Baker in a survey of Geoffrey Grigson's *New Verse*, a magazine which, Grigson acknowledged, 'came into existence because of Auden', wrote of the review's capacity as a nursery ground for new talent, 'including in addition to Auden, Day Lewis and Spender such new writers as Christoper Isherwood, Kenneth Allott … and William Plomer'. That Plomer – or for that matter Isherwood – never appeared in *New Verse* seems to have eluded his grasp. Indeed, Plomer mulishly refused to join a literary school or movement, having no particular aesthetic or political axe to grind. A hanger-on of Bloombury, though never quite a 'Bloomsberry', he joked about forming a 'Maida Vale Group' – a term first coined, I believe, by Virginia Woolf – with Joe Ackerley, Stephen Spender, and Air Commodore L.E.O. Charlton, a circle 'too deficient in team spirit, even to want, let alone attempt, to form anything like a group'. Spender, who had joined the Communist Party, admonished Plomer's failure to 'move beyond liberalism'. Plomer's ballad, 'Father and Son: 1939', hit Spender where it hurt:

With a firm grasp of half-truths, with political short-sight
With a belief we could disarm but at the same time fight,
And that only the Left Wing could ever be right
And that Moscow, of all places, was the sole source of light:
    Just like a young hopeful
    Between the wars.

'Literature has its battery hens,' Plomer wrote. 'I was a wilder fowl.' Therein lies the rub. 'An outsider from South Africa', as Bayley puts it, Plomer was, by definition, peripheral. His muddled ethnic identity, and to a lesser extent his sexual orientation, confounds matters. Race, sex, identity – contemporary poetry subsists on a diet of such shibolleths – Plomer should have more fans than he does (after all, he ticks all the 'representational' boxes). But there's a catch, and a gratifying one. Plomer does not write to tell us about himself. He knew, like all good poets, that 'selves', by and large, are radically boring, no matter how beleaguered by crises of racial identity, sexuality or whatever else. His commitment was to the life of the poem, to the discrete organisation of lines and stanzas, to character, to place: 'I'm incapable / Of starting the very least personality cult / I have freed myself at last from being me'. 'Austere, direct, free from emotional slither' – thus Ezra Pound set out his hopes for the poetry of the twentieth century. In the preface to the 1973 edition of his *Collected Poems*, Plomer decried the 'general tendency ... for the distorted personality of the artist to be valued more than the work of art itself', throwing in his lot with Pound in the 'move against poppycock'. In this regard he no doubt succeeded, but Plomer is nothing like Pound. No fan of the patchwork historical method, he could find sublimity anywhere (as Pound did once in a metro station). He had the remarkable ability to 'coax the delicate wings from the commonplace husk' – the quotidian was his bread and butter:

The commonplace needs no defence,
Dullness is in the critic's eyes,
Without a license life evolves
From some dim phase its own surprise …

On 15 March 1973, Plomer sent Lady Cholmondeley a short poem titled 'Painted on Darkness', collected here for the first time. Likely the last poem he ever wrote, it bears witness to his correctness, his clarity, his lyrical clout:

Each rose transmuted, sweeter than itself,
In pure vermilion stands out strange and new
Against the haunted glass intensified,
Painted on darkness, as a poem is.

IN AFRICA

THE DEATH OF A ZULU

The weather is mild
At the house of one of the dead.
There is fruit in the hands of his child,
There are flowers on her head.

Smoke rises up from the floor,
And the hands of a ghost
(No shadow darkens the door)
Caress the door-post.

Inside sits his wife, stunned and forsaken,
Too wild to weep;
Food lies uncooked at her feet, and is taken
By venturing fowls:
Outside, the dogs were asleep,
But they waken,
And one of them howls:
And Echo replies.

At last, with a sudden fear shaken,
The little child cries.

GANNETS AT UMDONI

Gannets plumb the wave like bombs:
Three fall white, and out of the wave one comes
Brown into air again, while shoals of fish
Undulate, like a stain upon the sea.
The gannets rise and turn, and then turn white and fall,
And flutter brown and wet out of the deep again.

ULA MASONDO'S DREAM

In a gorge titanic
Of the berg volcanic
A dark cave was hidden
Long untrodden.

There leopard and snake
And tawny partridge
Prey and are preyed on,
Unstartled by cartridge,
Where never a gun
Echoing shocks
The listening rocks;
Where in winter
When the granite crags
Receive the sun,
Far down, far down,
In the sombre forest
Under thin ice
The waters splinter
In flakes of fire,
And in shallow pools
The shadow of a hawk
Tense above the tree-tops
Quivers like a fish
Among the shadows
Of basking fishes.
When those parapets shimmer
In the morning in summer
The antelope turns
From the heat of the height
To a stream in the ferns,

Bounding unhurried
From sun to shadow:
There the lory wings scarlet
His way at noon; twilight
Rustles with bats;
And at dawn the cliff
Frowns with eagles;
There the wild cats
Crouch and tremble,
And hear the screams
Of the furtive jackal.

The cavern is hidden
In leaves and branches:
For centuries now
No avalanches
Have scarred the steep.
The cavern can keep
Its secret in stillness,
In darkness, enfolded
In the wild fig trees,
Whose sinews are moulded
To the curves of the stone,
And whose roots are thrust
In a crevice of dust,
Clinging tightly within
To the veins of the quartz,
And fed on the secret
And tasting-of-stone
Dews of the desert,
While their leaves unshaken
Are stirred by lizards,
A refuge for spiders,

An arbour for birds,
That gouge the soft fruit
And swoop into space
With thin stabs of music
In a hollow of silence.

On windless nights
When the cave is deserted
By the last baboon
The shafted radiance
Of the risen moon
Illumines like a lamp
The vaulted roof,
Where the moss is damp
And beaded with black
Dews bled from the rock,
Illumines like the ray
White and deific
Of an enormous Eye
This tongueless place
With light terrific.
In the flare and the hush
Appear the painted
Walls. Look, the art of
Hunters who were hunted
Like beasts by men!

Now the air is tainted
With a sudden whiff
Of distant carrion,
And the silence shrills
With the urgent quills
Of vultures soaring

From their look-out cliff,
Ready to feast
On dead man or dead beast.

But the silence returns
And moonlight floats,
And the Eye returns
To men before us
In time before ours,
Whose love and hunting
Are calcined in the blaze
Of light like chalk.

Far off, far off,
Where are the savage
Cities of the future?
When these colours fade
And lichens hang in their places,
When these forms lose their graces,
When these lines are not lines,
Blighted and bitten
By the gradual acid
Of rhythmic ages,
O up then and out
And over the placid
And azure sky of midday
Will take their way
These naked hunters
With their slow-stepping women
Stained with rose-ochre
Proudly proceeding
In prancing procession
With the eland and the gnu,

While each coloured
Courser canters
With the zebra and emu,
Giraffe and zebu,
Hunters and hunted
Flying forlorn,
Faint, faded, and few,
Far off, far off,
In the equal blue.

What are you doing,
Ula Masondo?
Do you follow the Bushmen?
Are you lost in the hollow
Root of the city?

A BASUTO COMING-OF-AGE

The winter sun, a distant roar of light,
Immensely sets, and far below this place
Cold on the plains the vast blue tides of night
Press on, and darken as they race.
Out of retreat, with dancing and with dirges,
Men bring a boy in whom a man emerges.

The new man sees anew the twisted aloes,
His father's house, his cattle in the shallows,
And up the hill a crowd of girls advancing
To carry him to drinking and to dancing –
His heart leaps up as he descends the steep,
For, where the boy slept, now the man shall sleep.

NAMAQUALAND AFTER RAIN

Again the veld revives,
Imbued with lyric rains,
And sap re-sweetening dry stalks
Perfumes the quickening plains;

Small roots explode in strings of stars,
Each bulb gives up its dream,
Honey drips from orchid throats,
Jewels each raceme;

The desert sighs at dawn –
As in another hemisphere
The temple lotus breaks her buds
On the attentive air –

A frou-frou of new flowers,
Puff of unruffling petals,
While rods of sunlight strike pure streams
From rocks beveined with metals;

Far in the gaunt karroo
That winter dearth denudes,
Ironstone caves give back the burr
Of lambs in multitudes;

Grass waves again where drought
Bleached every upland kraal,
A peach tree shoots along the wind
Pink volleys through a broken wall,

And willows growing round the dam
May now be seen
With all their traceries of twigs
Just hesitating to be green,

Soon to be hung with colonies
All swaying with the leaves
Of pendent wicker love-nests
The pretty loxia weaves.

THE SCORPION

Limpopo and Tugela churned
In flood for brown and angry miles
Melons, maize, domestic thatch,
The trunks of trees and crocodiles;

The swollen estuaries were thick
With flotsam, in the sun one saw
The corpse of a young negress bruised
By rocks, and rolling on the shore,

Pushed by the waves of morning, rolled
Impersonally among shells,
With lolling breasts and bleeding eyes,
And round her neck were beads and bells.

That was the Africa we knew,
Where, wandering alone,
We saw, heraldic in the heat,
A scorpion on a stone.

THE EXPLORER

Romantic subject of the Great White Queen,
See him advancing, whiskered and serene,
With helmet, spectacles, and flask of brandy
(That useful stimulant, he always keeps it handy),
Unmoved by cannibals, indifferent to disease;
His black frock-coat rocks sadly in the tropic breeze.

He never shows emotion, least of all surprise.
Here nothing meets his pale, protruding eyes
But big game, small game, fur and fin and feather,
And now he dreams of oatmeal, Scotland and the Flag,
The nimble corncrake in his native heather,
The handy corkscrew in his leather bag.

DIALOGUE
Nairobi

MAN TO GIRAFFE:
You walking Eiffel Tower, tall fantastic shape –

GIRAFFE TO MAN:
Go back to the gorillas, little trousered ape.

THE DEVIL DANCERS

In shantung suits we whites are cool,
Glasses and helmets censoring the glare;
Fever has made our anxious faces pale,
We stoop a little from the load we bear;

Grouped in the shadow of the compound wall
We get our cameras ready, sitting pensive;
Keeping our distance and our dignity
We talk and smile, though slightly apprehensive.

The heat strikes upward from the ground,
The ground the natives harden with their feet,
The flag is drooping on its bamboo pole,
The middle distance wavers in the heat.

Naked or gaudy, all agog the crowd
Buzzes and glistens in the sun; the sight
Dazzles the retina; we remark the smell,
The drums beginning, and the vibrant light.

Now the edge of the jungle rustles. In a hush
The crowd parts. Nothing happens. Then
The dancers stalk adroitly out on stilts,
Weirdly advancing, twice as high as men.

Sure as fate, strange as the mantis, cruel
As vengeance in a dream, four bodies hung
In cloaks of rasping grasses, turning
Their tiny heads, the masks besmeared with dung;

Each mops and mows, uttering no sound,
Each stately, awkward, giant marionette,
Each printed shadow frightful on the ground
Moving in small distorted silhouette;

The fretful pipes and thinly-crying strings,
The mounting expectation of the drums
Excite the nerves, and stretch the muscles taut
Against the climax – but it never comes;

It never comes because the dance must end
And soon the older dancers will be dead;
We leave by air tomorrow. How
Can ever these messages by us be read?

These bodies hung with viscera and horns
Move with an incomparable lightness,
And through the masks that run with bullocks' blood
Quick eyes aim out, dots of fanatic brightness.

Within the mask the face, and moulded
(As mask to face) within the face the ghost,
As in its chrysalis-case the foetus folded
Of leaf-light butterfly. What matters most

When it comes out and we admire its wings
Is to remember where its life began:
Let us take care – that flake of flame may be
A butterfly whose bite can kill a man.

THE BIG-GAME HUNTER

A big-game hunter opens fire once more,
Raconteur, roué, sportsman, millionaire and bore –
But only shoots his mouth off, knowing how
He's safer on a sofa than on far safari now.

THE RUINED FARM

A peaceful, archangelic sun
Sank low, grew larger to the sight,
And drew across each huge ravine
The huger curtains of the night;

Silence within the roofless house
Undid her hair and shook it free,
The footpad jackal passed her there,
And bats flew round the cactus tree;

Each quiet afternoon was bitter,
Was overcharged with warning,
And Silence waited where the snake lay coiled
And mocked at each mild, bright morning.

THE DEATH OF A SNAKE

Death and generation are both mysteries of nature, and somewhat
resemble each other – Marcus Aurelius

Bruised by a heel he strove to die,
In frantic spirals drilled the air,
Turned his pale belly upward to the sky
In coitus with death : and here and there
Scored in the dust quick ideographs of pain –
These, that the wind removed, in memory remain.

A TRANSVAAL MORNING

A sudden waking when a saffron glare
Suffused the room, and sharper than a quince
Two bird-notes penetrated there
Piercing the cloistral deep verandah twice.

The stranger started up to face
The sulphur sky of Africa, an infinite
False peace, the trees in that dry place
Like painted bones, their stillness like a threat.

Shoulders of quartz protruded from the hill
Like sculpture half unearthed; red dust,
Impalpable as cinnamon softly sifted, filled
With heaped-up silence rift and rut.

Again those two keen bird-notes! And the pert
Utterer, a moss-green thrush, was there
In the verandah-cave, alert,
About to flit into the breathless air.

The strangeness plucked the stranger like a string.
'They say this constant sun outstares the mind,
Here in this region of the fang, the sting,
And dulls the eye to what is most defined:

'A wild bird's eye on the *qui vive*
Perhaps makes vagueness clear and staleness new;
If undeceived one might not then deceive;
Let me', he thought, 'attain the bird's eye view.'

TUGELA RIVER

I

The river's just beyond that hill:
Drive up that track!

Look, isn't that someone standing there?

Yes, someone old and thin,
Some old witch perching there,
Standing on one wasted leg
With scaly skin, and taking snuff.
Unwanted, old and thin,
And waiting for the end,
She'll smell of ashes, and have no good news.
The skimpy rag she wears,
A cotton blanket once,
Protects her with its colour, not with warmth;
It has the dusty, ashen look
Of winter, scarcity, and drought.
Bones in a blanket, with a spark of life
Nothing by now can fan to flame,
Old hag, why don't you move?

It's not a woman, after all —
Only a thorn bush all disguised with dust!
Ah well, in this clear light
Things often are not what they seem,
Persons are often things,
Fear takes on form,
Delusions seem to have
The density of facts:
Kick one, and see!

44

It's just a thorn bush in a web of dust,
A statue of powder in this windless glare.
But, all the same, I shouldn't speak to it:
It might reply.
Silence itself might crack
Into an eerie cackle, dry and thin
As all this sapless winter grass,
Deriding us out of the lost past and out
Of what will be the past, when we are lost.

We've passed her now – or rather, *it*.
There, down the hill, the river in its bed,
Tugela River, seems as quiet
As this dead pythoness in her dusty fur.

White light, dry air, an even warmth
Make for well-being, tone and calm
The nerves, the blood.
No cloud, no breeze;
Clear as the focus of a burning-glass
But wholly bearable, the sun
Is fixed upon us like an eye.
We seem enclosed inside a vast
And flawless plastic dome
As for some new experiment.
We shall not know if we have passed the test,
We don't know what it is.

I feel we cannot fail.
The river in this still
Gold morning will renew our strength;
Reduced by drought
It does not show its own,

Only its constancy.
Look, turn off here, and park above that rock.

II

Tugela River! Thirty years ago
These same eyes saw you at this very place
Just at this time
Of winter, scarcity, and drought:
Not that you know or care;
But nothing is unrelated, wasted, lost.
There is a link
Between this river and that boy,
A boy obliged to learn
Subjects not mastered all at once –
Patience, and energy, and rage.

The hard earth cracked, the river shrank,
The boy came here because the river knew
Answers to questions.

Juiceless as straw, the glistening grass
Brittle and faintly gold
Waited for fire.

Then came the time of burning of the grass:
At night the veld-fires drew
Their mile-long arcs of jerking flame
Under the smoky stars.
Fences of dancing fire
Crackled like pistol shots,
Pricking new frontiers out
Into the passive dark.

It seemed the field by night
Of one of the those miscalled
Decisive battles of the world,
With cannon smoke and musket fire,
A master plan, and screams of pain
As some to-be-renowned outflanking move
Destroyed a long-established power
With crowns and crosses on its ancient pinnacles.
Morning revealed the hills mapped out
(Yesterday's straw-pale hills)
With empires painted black!

Burnt veld-grass had a sad and bitter smell
Like letters kept, then burnt,
Like battles fought, and lost –
No, battles fought and won!

III

Eastward and constant as a creed,
Tugela swam,
The winter river, much reduced,
Past shaped alluvial clean white sand,
Past stalks of maize upright but dead
In hillside patches poorly tilled
By dwellers under domes of reeds
Who by their poverty seemed to expiate
Their furious past.

Cool, cool Tugela slid
Haunted with unwritten myth,
Swam like a noble savage, dark
And muscular in shade, or clear
In the sun an emerald angel swam.

As sleek as oil Tugela poured,
And paused in pools,
And narrowing lapsed
Below the rigid erythrina trees
That held their carved and coral flowers
Like artifacts against the arid sky.

And farther down, down there,
Funnelled through channelled rocks
To rapids and cascades, kept up
A white roar of applause
In the still brightness of an empty day.

IV
Rivers of Europe with a cross of gold
In liquefaction at the inverted point
Of wavering dome or undulating spire,
Printed with dimnesses of trees
And redolent of mist and moss,
Reflect what looks like peace.

There, seated idols in a row,
The anglers on the bank
Catch something less than peace.
They never catch the gold reflected cross:
It ripples, breaks, re-forms, and melts.
No anglers here, fishing for peace.
Look at that pool, a glass
For nothing but the shadow of a rock.

It was a glass once for a Zulu youth –
I saw him standing on that rock
His fighting-sticks put by –

Who on a concertina improvised
A slow recurrent tune, subdued
By want of hope, yet with the stamping feet
The drums of hope
Beyond the horizon, and its just-heard song.

I know his family. They tell me he was found
Dying of inanition in the sun
On a road verge, while new cars
Hissed past like rockets
Loaded with white men hurrying like mad,
While he lay on the dark red earth
With all his youth subdued.

V
It is to be misled
To think his death was final, as to think
The river that you see, the dried-up grass,
Will stay like that;

Or that a race of men locked up and ruled
In a delusion built by psychopaths,
Locked up and staring at the floor
Between their patient feet,
Are there for good.

If, after thirty years, in winter calm
Tugela gliding as before might seem
Merely an unnavigable stream
Idling for ever in the gold
Dry atmosphere, remember this:
Patience erodes.

Here where we stand
Through the rich grass of summer there will pour
A press and pride of senseless force,
Roar like a mob, a tidal wave
Shaking its mane, and overturning rocks
Fulfil the promise of catastrophe.

When patience breaks, the sinews act,
Rage generates energy without end:
Tugela River, in the time of drums
And shouting of the war-dance flood
Will break a trance, as revolutions do,
Will promise order, and a future time
Of honey, beer, and milk.

THE WILD DOVES AT LOUIS TRICHARDT

Morning is busy with long files
Of ants and men, all bearing loads.
The sun's gong beats, and sweat runs down.
A mason-hornet shapes his hanging house.
In a wide flood of flowers
Two crested cranes are bowing to their food.
From the north today there is ominous news.

Midday, the mad cicada-time.
Sizzling from every open valve
Of the overheated earth
The stridulators din it in –
Intensive and continuing praise
Of the white-hot zenith, shrilling on
Toward a note too high to bear.

Oven of afternoon, silence of heat.
In shadow, or in shaded rooms,
This face is hidden in folded arms,
That face is now a sightless mask,
Tree-shadow just includes those legs.
The people have all lain down, and sleep
In attitudes of the sick, the shot, the dead.

And now in the grove the wild doves begin,
Whose neat silk heads are never still,
Bubbling their coolest colloquies.
The formulae they liquidly pronounce
In secret tents of leaves imply
(Clearer than man-made music could)
Men being absent, Africa is good.

IN JAPAN

HOTEL MAGNIFICENT (YOKOHAMA, 1927)

If you long to mingle with Cosmopolitans in Yokohama amidst gorgeous
Oriental pageantry, fill out and mail the information blank below
– Contemporary American advertisement

Where stout hunters unbamboozled by the stoutest of bamboos
Suck icy liquors up through straws or strut in patent-leather shoes,
While tourists of both sexes bandy-legged or bald as bandicoots
Hobnob with Hollywood's who's-who or dally with cheroots,
Stranger, look round, or stand and listen to the band.

Japan, they say that Kipling said, is 'not a sahib's land',
But *si sahib requiris, circumspice* in the well-planned grand
Brand-new Hotel Magnificent whose highly-polished floors
Reflect both millionaires and brassy pseudo-Jacobean cuspidors.

Descend with despatch to the Daimyo Dining Room
('Takes the tired tourist back to stirring Feudal Days'),
Fashioned all in Burmese teak and like an Aztec magnate's tomb
Well it has deserved a drunken baseball-champion's praise.

'Old-world craft,' with New World craftiness
The new prospectus says, 'continually ply
Beneath these very windows' – but the naked eye
Sees nothing more than motor-boats beneath a smoky sky.

The pergola pillars on the roof are hollow,
Made of cement and steel and topped with whirring cowls
To ventilate the kitchens ninety feet below
And a corridor to the ballroom where a loud-voiced gossip prowls:

'She says they say they may go from here to San Diego
Or Spain by aeroplane or out into the blue;
On the fat wife of a dago seed-pearls look like small sago
But she certainly asserts he is a personage in Peru.'

Here East meets West to the strains of *The Mikado*
Born kicking from the strings of a Filipino band
Whose members have an air of languor and bravado,
And one a Russian emerald lucent on his hand,
A trophy of the ups and downs, the switchback way we go,
Pressed upon a supple finger by an exile starving in the snow.

The band strikes up again and from bedroom and bridge-table
In this modern Tower of Babel people glide towards the door;
The band bursts out anew, and a wistful nasal whining
With hypnotic syncopation fills the ballroom's glossy floor
With two-backed beasts side-stepping, robots intertwining,
Trying to work a throwback, to be irresponsible once more.

JAPONAISERIE

O la douce vie insensée!
The early sun accentuates
Green lettuces on rime-white soil
With shadows glowing blue.

A sparrow leaves a springboard twig
And powdered sugar falls: look up
Where arsenal chimneys trace
Sky-writing slow on frozen air.

The sacred Fuji, pale as pearl,
Is ruled across with telegraph wires –
Moi mandarin, toi mandarine,
Nous irons, souriant un peu.

AT LAKE CHUZENJI

'The best July resort in the whole Far East'
So he was told, the stout Bombay Greek
Watching the water, clear and still as aspic.

The yacht race this morning looks like yesterday,
White isosceles triangles on parallels sliding
Passing and repassing, he wonders to what end.

V within V behind a motor boat
The splay waves spread and waver, a German lady swims,
Down comes the rain and voices interpenetrate.

'We ought to go and see that beastly waterfall.'
'Who is this young man that follows her round?'
'Three hearts.' 'And you?' 'I pass.' 'What's yours?'

A sudden yearning for an evening with geisha
Cruises along his hardening arteries,
But sadly he turns his broad back on the lake,

Resigned to missing intimacy with Japanese joys,
To no longer being young, and to not being free
From his wife, his daughter, his hotel, or propriety.

WHITE AZALEAS

Mats of woven grass
  In the lighted room
    Where he lay in bed;

All at once he heard
  The audible-by-night
    Bamboo waterfall;

Shadows of the trees
  Were moving on the ground
    Underneath the moon.

Midori came back
  With a hiss of silk,
    And knelt upon the floor,

In her golden hand
  A branch of white azaleas
    Crystal-dropped with dew.

THE GINGKO TREE

Chrome-yellow in the blue,
    Tremolando tree,
Flute-like aquarelle,
    Pure fragility.
    When the sun
Faded in a misty wind
    Branches spun,
    Scattered clear
Propaganda, quickly thinned
    Turning twigs,
    Leaves untwirled –
Parasol or pamphleteer.

AUTUMN NEAR TOKYO

A pear, a peach, a promenade,
September sheds the first red leaf
Between tall millet rows
A stooping woman reaps.

Persimmons fatten overhead
And thin blue smoke aspires
To fade into the paler sky.
Still hardly cool the evening comes.

A dusky freshness and the sweet
And musky cheapness of a cigarette
Hang on the fading air. The old
Are thinking of the past.

Emphatic through the mist
Twangs the strong samisen;
Those taut strings struck
In a light top room

Are struck for us, the young!
Arrows into the night
That bowstring song lets fly,
Our longings to be strong!

THOUGHTS ON THE JAPANESE INVASION OF CHINA

Taut paper and clean wood enclose
    A neat, sweet domestic place
Where slant sun and magic snows
    Alter the shadow on a well-loved face.

Warm wine in a little cup,
    A red leaf fell, a white sleeve fluttered,
Morning smoke was wafted up,
    More, more was felt than uttered.

Why, then why the rape of a child,
    The lidless eyes, the screaming man,
The ricefield village all defiled
    To a cold, elaborate, zestful plan?

Because shy fingers end in claws,
    Behind soft lips are teeth that bite,
And a vast uneasy longing roars
    Up like a bomber through the night.

From the gods was stolen the seed of fire,
The Dragon flew in the face of the Sun –
One god is Hope, a hardened liar,
Another is Love, the unconquered one.

A MOMENT OF PEACE

Lulled on the Yellow Sea
    Long lacquered afternoons
Idly loll the refugees
    From the maniac typhoons.

Muffled rolling satin deep,
    Early night, a star breeze
Stirs the peonies on the slope
    And the sleeping Annamese.

Underneath the folded sail
    Its photograph in monochrome
Wavers, and the evening lull
    Saddens, like a dream of home.

IN GREECE

DISTICHS

from Greek originals

I

Curse you, plane-tree, for your leafiness —
The girls fetching water can no longer be seen.

II

Want me as I want you, and as I love, love me —
Or the time may come that you'll love me when I want you no more.

PERSEPHONE

Pluto in a black barouche
    Axle-deep in asphodel
Busbied and in Hessian boots
    Was preceded by a farouche
Arab horses with postilions epauletted and in suits
    Of the livery of Hell.

From a small cloisonné box
    He took a pinch of best rappee
While his four Dalmatian hounds
    Prancing spotted on the rocks
Drew attention to a lady, seeing whom he murmured
      'Zounds!
    This was what I hoped to see.'

Proserpine was in a bonnet
    And a yellow grenadine
With a high Directoire waist
    And silver spangles on it,
Muslined and beribboned, shod with sandals criss-
      cross laced –
    Merveilleuse or muscadine?

Echo mimics vain alarms,
    Every leaf and flower fades,
Whips crack, sable harness tightens,
    Close he pinions two white arms,
While the swaying equipage down ways a ghastly
      balefire brightens
    Carries sorrow to the shades.

THE RUINS

Snapped off and earthquake-scattered
Segments of Corinthian columns lie
Fluted like celery-stalks in stone
Buff-biscuit on the desert grey.

Some stand, supporting yet
Fragments of pediments soon to fall.
Acanthus capitals can be kicked
Out of the sand like fossils. Surely

No moral need be drawn from this?
Bright poisonous gourds have coiled
Over the vast cylinders, but these
Small wild musk-melons ought to quench our thirst.

STILL LIFE

Rosined strings and gourd-shaped rosewood,
A bow on that taut gut, drawn over those would
Cause vinous tones as unto eyes unshut the dawn renews
Things back to shapes, to amber stones, from slumber hues.
Urned on plain glass cool grapes unleaved repose,
Vase, scroll, and those ice-green in clearness tremellose,
Claret with umber mute one more warm touch refuse.

THE LAND OF LOVE

Kalirrhoë Kalogerópoulos, widow, keeps a café
At the supposed site of the Serangeion baths,
A small pink house under a fragrant fig tree
Built into the cliff-face and reached by goat-track paths.

'The Land of Love' is the name of the café;
It is well named, for the terrace night by night is
Frequented by at least two or three pairs of lovers
And the bathing-booths below are also Aphrodite's.

In the evening one enjoys thin resined wine, then
(A beggar with a guitar going by in the gloom)
The black currant-grapes that are eaten by bunches,
Red mullet with pepper, and a powdered *loukoum*.

Loukas, Vasili, and Nestor, municipal clerks,
Used to come here by tram when melons were ripest;
Loukas was drowned, diving among the moon-flakes,
And Vasili shot Nestor on account of a typist.

THREE PINKS

Crisp hair with a faint smell like honey
Hived by fierce bees under a fallen column in a pinewood,
A liquor of wild oleanders in a limestone gully –
Although it is summer there is snow on Parnassus –
Crisp hair awoke me, brushing my cheek.

Open your eyes, undo those modest fringes
Under the eyebrow-arches, wide, Byzantine, black,
White-wine coloured eyes in a rose-tan skin,
Antique young eyes! Smile, my primitive,
Fill the hushed air with amusement and secrecy,
And you need not, with such fine teeth, forbear to yawn –
And with such sweet breath.

                Still half awake
We shall get up together from the bed
And with arms interlaced cross to the window
(The early morning is cool and heavenly),
Then standing mutely look out over a quiet
Aspect of Athens, rococo houses and stucco
With a cypress or two in the middle distance
Like marks of exclamation at such tranquillity.

See, in the exsiccate light of Attica
The pepper-tree garden where last night by full moon
An old woman disturbed our intimacy
To sell us three pinks with long stems.

See now, the Acropolis is still unsunned.
Forestall dawn with yet one more kiss,
Last of the night or first of the day –
Whichever way one may chance to choose to regard it.

CORFU

The fig divides where mortar bound
The bastion and the parapet,
Fennel and sage and grasses wave,
No gunsmoke drifts across the bay,
This is a view without a war.

Across the old fortezza fall
The crystal rulings of the rain,
The moon above Albania burns
Fitful as a brigand's fire,
And no boat passes out to sea.

Cloud-light dazzles with cliffs of peace
The tranced Homeric afternoons,
The sea tumbles pale and dark,
A gull wheels, and a clock counts four
Not heard by ears that earth has filled.

Empty at night the shuttered square,
Lightning shakes the tall pink town,
Turkish, Venetian, English hearts
Have stopped beneath the struggling wind,
The wrestling trees and wetted walls.

In lamplight the magnolia leaves
Blink wet with rain and metal-bright,
At the old fort the lighthouse beams
Its constant warning north and south
Smoothly, to keep Ulysses from the rocks.

ANOTHER COUNTRY

'Let us go to another country,
Not yours or mine,
And start again.'

   To another country? Which?
   One without fires, where fever
   Lurks under leaves, and water
   Is sold to those who thirst?
   And carry drugs or papers
   In our shoes to save us starving?

'Hope would be our passport;
The rest is understood.'

   Deserters of the vein
   And true continuousness,
   How should we face on landing
   The waiting car, in snow or sand,
   The alien capital?
   Necessity forbids.

(Not that reproachful look!
So might violets
Hurt an old heart.)

   This is that other country
   We two populate,
   Land of a brief and brilliant
   Aurora, noon and night,
   The stratosphere of love
   From which we must descend,

And leaving this rare country
Must each to his own
Return alone.

IN ENGLAND

THE SILENT SUNDAY

From the bandstand in the garden on the hill
Where workless seamen moped on benches
And shrieking children worked the swings
The wide curve of the estuary can be seen.

Half-way down the hill a murder case
Once drew idle crowds to stare
Over the mottled laurels in the garden of an inn,
And a newspaper stood up on end
And moved unsteadily, urged by the wind,
Like a child that learns to walk.

That busy world of cars and bungalows,
Who would have thought that it would stop so soon?
Fissures appeared in football fields
And houses in the night collapsed.
The Thames flowed backward to its source,
The last trickle seen to disappear
Swiftly, like an adder to its hole,
And here and there along the river-bed
The stranded fish gaped among empty tins;
Face downward lay the huddled suicides
Like litter that a riot leaves.

They say some women lived for weeks
Hidden in bushes on the common, then drew lots
And ate each other. Now
A sunny mist hangs over everything.
An almond tree suggests that this is spring
But on the right an oak retains its leaves.

Where are the sea-birds? Why no gulls?
All drowned when the oil-tanks burst?
Water chuckles from a broken pipe.

A LOST FACE

To seek a lost or missed face, and not trace it
Slides a screen of clear glass across street, grass and vista,
As for a huntsman killing for hunger not fun
Leaf and twig cruelly detailed and motionless
Seem in the know, conspirational,
Hiding fawn pelt of beast or grain-fattened bird
Dearer by disappearance, needed by the trigger finger,
The sharp-eyed stomach, and the children at home.

Seeking to trace the lost face, it seems untrue
That the tides of ourselves, in hats, shoes, and coats,
Ghosts lent substance, precarious hurriers
Whom death teases, neglects or surprises,
Should be able to conceal such features as those –
But look at the shallows: they shelter a kingfisher.

Hereabouts the treasure was buried
But the keen spade dredges up nothing but earth.
It is time to go home – unless suddenly the steel
Strikes metal, and vibrates like a tuning-fork.

SEPTEMBER EVENING: 1938

As the golden grass burns out
In a cooling ash of dew
The lovers disembrace
And face the evening view.

The long plain down
Shaped like a thigh
Slopes towards the sea,
And away up in the sky

Too small to be heard
A purposeful silver spark
Bright in the sun's last rays
Glides eastward into the dark;

Plain as a stack of hay
In the valley at their feet
A primitive small church
Looks simple, strong, and neat:

Inside a wattled fold
An unsafe flock of sheep
Stand, stir, or lie
Fleece against fleece asleep;

Lights in a bungalow,
A constant hum of cars;
Mallow flowers in the grass;
One or two stars.

With the fading day
All has grown clear:
All is felt to be vital
And infinitely dear.

Looking round, the girl thinks
'How precious to me
My home and my work and each thing
I can touch and can see,

'George's navy-blue suit,
And my white linen dress,
And the way that his eyebrows grow –
This is my happiness!'

And he, clasping her hand,
More grave than before,
Says, 'Yes, I will fight
From no lust for war

'But for all that has gone to make
Us, and this day.'
Then arm in arm along the path
Silent they saunter away.

HEADLINE HISTORY

GRAVE CHARGE IN MAYFAIR BATHROOM CASE,
ROMAN REMAINS FOR MIDDLE WEST,
GOLFING BISHOP CALLS FOR PRAYERS,
HOW MURDERED BRIDE WAS DRESSED,

BOXER INSURES HIS JOIE-DE-VIVRE,
DUCHESS DENIES THAT VAMPS ARE VAIN,
DO WOMEN MAKE GOOD WIVES?
GIANT AIRSHIP OVER SPAIN,

SOPRANO SINGS FOR FORTY HOURS,
COCKTAIL BAR ON MOORING MAST,
'NOISE, MORE NOISE!' POET'S LAST WORDS,
COMPULSORY WIRELESS BILL IS PASSED,

ALLEGED TRUMP BLOWN YESTERDAY,
TRAFFIC DROWNS CALL TO QUICK AND DEAD,

CUP TIE CROWD SEES HEAVENS OPE,
'NOT END OF WORLD', SAYS WELL-KNOWN RED.

TATTOOED

On his arms he wears
Diagrams he chose,
A snake inside a skull,
A dagger in a rose,

And the muscle playing
Under the skin
Makes the rose writhe
And the skull grin.

He is one who acts his dreams
And these emblems are a clue
To the wishes in his blood
And what they make him do,

These signs are truer
Than the wearer knows:
The blade vibrates
In the vulnerable rose,

Anthers bend, and carmine curly
Petals kiss the plunging steel,
Dusty with essential gold
Close in upon the thing they feel.

A CHARM AGAINST TROUBLE

The wand that speaks and the silent fruit
Have been won from the difficult tree,
And armed with these the winner can face
The evil eye that sees from afar,
The lunatic wind in the empty place,
The northern lights and the falling star,
And the gunfire thudding across the sea.

To hold that egg-like fruit in the palm,
To be even touched by that willowy shoot
Gives life, ends grief, and nullifies harm,
For the roots of the tree go down to the lake
Where we all began, where we all belong.
Turn to the world, traveller. Take
What the sap forms; the stick is in song.

UNITY

A white stalk of uprooted sedge
Touches an aromatic nerve,
Recalls the past, as that recalled
Ancestral voices living still
In figures walking over graves.

A bunch of elderberries dark,
Or branches broken by the wind,
Are joined with duty and desire
And Nostradamus mocking Time
Remembering future happenings.

A WALK IN WÜRZBURG

Passing a dull red college block
Of the bygone, full-fed, Kaiser time,
When the tribal mercury welled up
Ready to burst, is to wonder if inside
That institute some intent and hairy head,
Bored by the strut of the show-off turkey-cock,
Through steel-rimmed ovals used at that time perhaps
To peer with love, pure love, of finding out;

Is to wonder who now may be tunnelling there
For an unknown vein, or perhaps with the sifting hand
Of an archaeologist-in-reverse
Dredging towards a treasure the future hides.
Bombs broke the wigged Baroque only yards away,
But his thoughtful back would be that of a sage
Averted from fractured dreams, unhealable wounds,
Revenges, ruined walls, undruggable nerves.

By chance to see an inconspicuous plaque
On that otherwise unadorned wall, is to learn
That here, right here, a miracle struck
Which altered us all – as Gutenberg did,
Daguerre, or Freud; is to feel what the pious feel,
Quite carried away to find they face
Unawares a place of sublime prestige,
Where a saint flared out of the chrysalid stage.

Not to have known about this! That here,
That nowhere else in the wasteful, wilful,
Death-wishing world, here Röntgen focused his ray
And the eye first saw right through the skin,

So that now without knives we see what is wrong
Or is going to be wrong. We still need a ray
To coax the delicate wings from the commonplace husk
And detect why the horde we are destroys itself.

from **READING IN THE GARDEN**

Twitching upon a Mexican marigold
With lightest palpation, a pale
Chalk-blue, its tendril probe
Siphoning summer thin as a thread.

Overhead something obsessive,
A skating, shimmering nebula hangs –
Midges involved in a tribal dance:
What can one do but watch?

Reception is good for the senses today:
To clear the chuckle, whistle,
Clatter of mad glad starlings,
Bossy and glossy, plebeian.

It is not easy in an August garden
To read with attention. Two books
Wait beside me, neither a flower
I feel drawn to sip.

LIME-FLOWER TEA

The esplanade empty, closed at this time
    The gates of the park;
The sea waveless, only a murmur
    In the formless dark
Of a night in winter; frost fusing
    Glass beads of drifted snow,
Trashy remnants of a white glare
    One dazzling day ago.

Frost hardens, glazes, grips; on glass
    Will damascene
Traceries tonight of ferns.
    A plain screen
Of fog has curtained off the sea.
    Street lamps illuminate
A livid emptiness, and one man,
    Only one, walking late.

He stops walking, stands then, vaguely gazing
    Is amazed to hear
Gentle flutings of seabirds,
    Unseen but near –
Communings of pure confidence,
    Intimations of their ease
And of a separate togetherness
    No arctic night could freeze.

Each flute-note has made him think
    Of his own life –
Quiet years with a neurotic
    Childless wife:

On a winter night, when needling frost
    In total silence etches ferns,
He to her like a seabird speaks,
    She, wingless, to him turns.

His walk alone at night she understands
    And the unsaid;
In the warm room she'll pour out,
    Before bed,
Delicately, lime-flower tea;
    Together they will sip and dream,
Sad and content, both drugged
    By the lost summer in the scented steam.

THE BUNGALOWS

In lofty light the towers dissolve
Of yellow elms this tranquil day,
Crumble in leisurely showers of gold
All Turneresque in bright decay.

The elms disperse their leaves upon
A nineteen-thirty builder's row
Of speculative dwellings, each
An unassuming bungalow.

Like concave shells, or shades, or shields
That guard some life or light aloof,
Like hands that cup a flame, or keep
Some frail and captured thing, each roof.

If high-pitched hopes have gone to roost
Where low-pitched roofs so smoothly slope
Perhaps these autumn rays diffuse
A deeper anodyne than hope.

Between the vast insanities
That men so cleverly invent
It may be here, it may be here,
A simulacrum of content.

Though separate only from the road
By five-foot hedge and ten-foot lawn
Each semi-isolationist
Seems almost from the world withdrawn,

Except that from a roof or two
Those thin and wand-like aerials rise
That suck like opium from the air
Bemusement for the ears and eyes.

The denizens of each hermitage,
Of 'Nellibert' and 'Mirzapore',
Bird-watchers all, in love with dogs,
Are primed with useful garden-lore:

Cabbage the emblem of their life –
Yet mauve the michaelmas-daisy glows
And under reddening apples gleams
A pearly, pure, belated rose.

Begrudging vulgar fantasy
To cheap and ordinary homes,
Discrimination might deplore
That concrete frog, those whimsy gnomes,

Nor see them as blind tribute to
The rule of dreams, or as a last
Concession to the irrational,
The old, wild, superstitious past.

The commonplace needs no defence,
Dullness is in the critic's eyes,
Without a license life evolves
From some dim phase its own surprise:

Under these yellow-twinkling elms,
Behind these hedges trimly shorn,
As in a stable once, so here
It may be born, it may be born.

BEFORE THE CRASH

Caught sight of from the car
(Just before the crash)
On the river bank
    Against a hanging cliff of bronze
    A great white colony
    Of resting and of nesting swans.

In marble attitudes
(Distant, as things are
Living their own lives)
    The swans, arranged in twos and threes,
    Were doing nothing; we
    Were doing eighty – and with ease.

Seen also from the car,
Minutes and miles along,
Flames in a ballet stretch
    Enormous up from straw and trash
    In frenzy to attain
    The coda – just a little ash.

Tempi of swans and fires,
Cars, and suns beyond
Furnace-roaring suns
    No man will ever hear – in space
    These harmonize, none are
    Winners or losers in a race.

TWO ELEGIES

I – THE SHORTEST DAY

Fume of fine food and room-warmed wine
In a warm high room above the sea;
Hint of narcissus in the air displaced
By a woman moving; two men with cigars;
Windows wide open on a frosted, waiting day –
The shortest day. Aroma of living, savour of being,
Of well-being, chemistry of sympathy, accord,
Life at a height, warm life – and yet
      All is not well.

Today there is no horizon, the increasing towns
Are all one town, stopped only by the shore.
Along the edge of the water's vast taboo
Cars pause, that have bred like flies, and buzz
On the puzzling glass of winter, by that cut off
From the white, quiet, boatless, motorless,
Shortest-day sea. Drifts of resentful cars
Edge out, drone off, freeing from their dull gaze
      The waveless sea.

The sea, a breathing opal, lifts and lets fall
And lifts again a crushing indolent shoal
Of coppery flakes from the smudged and smouldering sun;
Out there the stillest day; out there
The engine of the sea is idling, giving
Now and then an undulant shudder, raising
A wavering edge; then the desolate sigh and hiss
Of the merest wavelet, an accent on silence
      Filling the room.

Up there just then no talk of the past, of its
Folly and mania, impulses, appetites, accidents;
Frenzies of adolescence; journeys in vain;
Anxiety throbbing like a disease;
The axe of bereavement; the bait of hope
On the hook of failure; electric delights;
Trust growing slowly. Physical beauty still
Imbues and graces all three. It cannot make
   Plain joys hold fast.

Out there horizontal calm; yes, but a
Stage for horrors performed – only the sea's
Are not acted, are real; they continue.
Each in that room, on a different stage
Or ocean voyage, was geared by a compromise,
The woman a sail that carried a man along,
One man by devotion powered and steered,
The other set on a predetermined course
   Of no return.

Each was involved in rhythms not one
Had foreseen or intended. The woman could ever
Taste again the dreamy mutuality known
To the young. The watchful man had a lasting
Love that was duty, whole-time. The other
Was already a long way off, and spoke
To the others over a chasm. (The courage of somewhat
Privileged persons may merit more praise
   Than it may get.)

The shortest day is soon over. Afternoon
Hardly occurs. Day's pearl dulls. The not much
Uprisen sun has gone blurred and glimmering by.

From that high room soon to disperse,
Now from the window they watch from its frost-cocoon
The sun float free – bare, huge and red.
'Just look at the sun!' 'But who can tell
What it possibly means? Does it mean STOP
        Or DANGER – which?'

Later a little, livid, the lulled sea slid
One way, from east to west, a satin dyed
With ebbing light, endlessly drawn along
From day's vat into the dark. Great liquid lake,
It is a distillation of the drowned. Even just then
Perhaps, not far away, and quite unseen
Was entering into it, too intent to feel
Its venomous ache, some loneliest, dowdiest suicide
        Waist-deep, alone.

The woman is not in the room, has left like a scarf
Her trail of narcissus. The man has gone, for whom
In marriage is order. The other looks out, alone,
And the calm is for him a terrible pause.
For some there is no sedation, not in a high warm room
Above the December sea; in company, they are apart,
And homeless at home; and love, of which they hear much,
Is a distant light. Facing the sea now, he
        Dreams of the drowned.

Of that suicide, received in a total embrace
By water, to be translated into the basic
Language of being, reassumed into the unending
Dance of the elements, the chain of reviving,
Dissolving shapes, needs, impulses. In that
How can he possibly find what some may suppose

94

Exists, and presume to call a 'meaning'?
Who on earth can read a language
          Quite beyond words?

If men are made in the image of God, then
No two being alike, each is a different glint
Of a diamond much flawed, or a cheque drawn
On an inexhaustible account, a syllable
In a story still being written. Unending millions
Of try-outs are tried out as if for a purpose
And then discarded, dissolved, rejected;
Millions of differing, vanishing images are what
          God makes man in.

How many have vanished at sea! A slave ship at noon
Unchains only the sick; prone with fever and despair,
Ebony giants lose value; robed only in their last sweat,
Still breathing, still seeing, are jettisoned to sharks.
Or on some calm spring night breaks out a screech
Of grinding metal, waterfalls, fire bells; in cabins tilting
Bewildered children are snatched up from sleep
By love as the ship sinks. But there is no help.
          They are not saved.

Up a vertical wave a raft swoops, against it
Three sailors are snails glued on a wall;
False hope is the force that holds them there;
They were armed; they are unarmed now; one slips,
The last two lose hold; the raft rears up,
The last one now, as the raft plunges, is gone.
What is it all for? Now against a new cliff
Of ice-green water hangs a blackboard with no lesson –
          The raft is blank.

The shortest day has sunk in the longest night,
In a coma of cold. The watcher alone up there
About to exclude the dark, must turn to face
A darkness within; but now sees one small light
Putting out to sea, with the vibrant vigilant beat
Of the motor of one small boat. To be so slight
Seems impertinent, in the knowledge that out from here
To the rocks of eternal ice, all is water
          And half is night.

Life isn't only a slave ship, a shipwreck; it's also
An outgoing boat with an outboard motor at night
Pitter-pattering off with a confident impetus
Into the dark with its light, into the frost with its heat,
Into the end of the night. The atlas avers
That the place remains, that turbulent place,
And the name, that marvellous name, persists;
Yes, even that soul up there was bound for his own
          Cape of Good Hope.

II – THE TASTE OF THE FRUIT

*In memory of the poet Ingrid Jonker, who was found dead by night at
Sea Point, Cape Town, in July, 1965; and of Nathaniel Nakasa, the
South African writer, who died by suicide in the United States in the
same month.*

Where a dry tide of sheep
Ebbs between rocks
In a miasma of dust,
Where time is wool;
He is not there.

Where towers of green water
Crash, re-shaping
White contours of sand,
Velvet to a bare foot;
She is not there.

Where pride in modesty,
Grace, neatness,
Glorify the slum shack
Of one pensive woman;
He is not there.

Where one fatherly man
Waited with absolute
Understanding, undemanding
Hands full of comfort;
She is not there.

Where sour beer and thick smoke,
Lewdness and loud

Laughter half disguise
Hope dying of wounds;
He is not there.

Where meat-fed men are idling
On a deep stoep,
Voicing disapproval
Of those who have 'views';
She is not there.

Where with hands tied
They wrestle for freedom;
Where with mouth stopped
They ripen a loud cry;
He is not there.

Where intellectuals
Bunch together to follow
Fashions that allow for
No private exceptions;
She is not there.

He, who loved learning,
Nimbly stood up to
The heavyweight truth;
For long years in training
He is not there,

She was thought childlike
But carried the iron
Seeds of knowledge and wisdom;
Where they now flower,
She is not there.

A man with no passport,
He had leave to exile
Himself from the natural
Soil of his being,
But none to return.

She, with a passport,
Turned great eyes on Europe.
What did she return to?
She found, back home, that
She was not there.

Now he is free in
A state with no frontiers,
But where men are working
To undermine frontiers,
He is not there.

'My people,' in anguish
She cried, 'from me have rotted
Utterly away.' Everywhere
She felt rejected;
Now she is nowhere.

Where men waste in prison
For trying to be fruitful,
The first fruit is setting
Themselves fought for;
He will not taste it.

Her blood and his
Fed the slow, tormented
Tree that is destined

To bear what will be
Bough-bending plenty.

Let those who savour
Ripeness and sweetness,
Let them taste and remember
Him, her, and all others
Secreted in the juices.

LATE POEMS (1966–73)

STONES OF ARGYLL

Clans, claymores, cackle about battles,
Jacobites, Covenanters, noisy Knox,
that tall thin nympho Queen of Scots —
all those, to a petrologist, are trash,
newspaper stuff. Newspapers are used
for lighting fires or wrapping fish.

You pick up scraps of gossip out of books:
that's history. Prehistory for me!
Don't misunderstand me if I say 'That's gneiss',
I'm looking at 300 million years,
at how the world was made. Stones
are what I mean by concrete poetry.

The tide receding from this beach
makes every stone fresher than paint —
cake-like conglomerate, black basalt,
pink granite, purplish andesite,
quartzite, felsite. Gorgeous most
these reddish jaspers with their soapy feel.

A CHURCH IN BAVARIA

Everything flows
  upward over
    chalk–white walls
      with the ordered freedom
        of a trellised creeper
      wreathed and scrolled
    in a densely choral
  anthem of ornament.

Nimble angels
  poise above
    in attitudes,
      huge–limbed prophets
        banner–bearded,
      giant apostles,
    mitred titans
  exemplify
authority,
  their garments ribbed
    in whorls and folds,
      corrugations
        of pearly grace,
      sea–shell volutions
    turned by ages and
  oceans of prayer.

Visions of Paradise
    pivot their rolling
        eyeballs upwards,
            their lips issue
                garlands of praise,
            flexible
        they bend from narrow
    waists, and raise
smooth rounded arms
    with hands adoring
        or holding golden
            instruments,
                long fingers fingering
            tingling harps,
        long trumpets sounding
    triumph unending.

Everything flowers
    in aspiration
        to an imagined
            culmination,
                the athlete spirit's
            endless training
        gives ecstatic
    buoyant lightness,
all aspires as
    shaped and soaring

white and ring-dove
grey and gilded
formal figures
in a sacred dance.

What does all this
joyful brilliance
have to do with
cults obsessed with
guilt and sin,
a punishing angry
vindictive God?
Where's that hard
right-angled object
the Cross, with Victim
blanched by torture,
dead, with blood?

Here the focal
point discloses
a seated Virgin,
her covered head
at a fond angle
in accord with
all this swaying
court of images,
looking down
benign and gentle
at the incredible
fact, her Child.

Everything sings
in snowy stillness,
in marble wonder,
in formal myth,
believed because
impossible,
believed as only
a poem can be,
the anti-fact
of a holy spore
spreading the Word
unsaid before.

Everything bends
to re-enact
the poem lived,
lived not written,
the poem spoken
by Christ, who never
wrote a word,
saboteur
of received ideas
who rebuilt Rome
with the words he
never wrote;
whether sacred,
whether human,
himself a sunrise
of love enlarged,
of love, enlarged.

A CASUAL ENCOUNTER

In memory of Cavafy, 1863–1933

They met, as most these days do,
among streets, not under leaves; at night;
by what is called chance, some think
predestined; in a capital city, latish;
instantly understanding, without words,
without furtiveness, without guilt,
each had been, without calculation, singled out.

Wherever it was they had met,
without introduction, before drifting this way,
beneath lamps hung high, casting
cones of radiance, hazed with pale dust,
a dry pollenous mist that made
each warm surface seem suede, the sense of touch
sang like a harp; the two were alone.

To be private in public added oddness,
out of doors in a city with millions
still awake, with the heard obbligato
of traffic, that resolute drone,
islanding both, their destination
the shadow they stood in. The place
should perhaps be defined.

But need it? Cliff walls of warehouses;
no thoroughfare; at the end a hurrying
river, dragonish; steel gates locked;
emptiness. Whatever they said
was said gently, was not written down,

not recorded. Neither had need
even to know the other one's name.

Nor do you need to know any more
of an hour so far off, so far,
it may be, from what turns you on.
They, with peacefullest smiles at a rare
Befriedigung, parted, breathing the gold-
dusted, denatured air like the pure
air of some alp : nor met ever again.

Is that all? To you it may seem
a commonplace episode. Once was a man
who might not have thought so. To him
(an old photograph hides his neck clamped
in a high stiff white collar, on his pale face
a false-looking moustache) let me dedicate
this moth-winged encounter, to him, to Cavafy himself.

NO IDENTITY

Against the name of the place we mean to move to
The guidebook bleakly rules *No identity*:
What Doctor Pevsner means is absence of ancient
Or markworthy buildings.
        What he implies
Is a shallowly-rooted community, a huddlement
Of not very settled commuters, interspersed with retired
Couples, tending to dwindle to widows,
Little communal sense or parish pride,
And the usual private or commonplace fears
Like that of being moved to some distant branch
Of one's place of work, or of cold old age.

But if a triumphal arch were to welcome us
What better inscription than this, *No identity*?
We are not the sort who wish to reflect prestige
From a rare environment. By possessing antiques
Or using the newest things we feel no need
To reinforce our own identity; at our age
That seems unambiguous enough.
         My need
As a poet (not every poet's) is this –
To be immersed in a neutral solution, which
Alone provides an interim, until through the grey
Expectant film invisible writing comes clean.

No identity can be a desirable thing:
To have a face with features noticed less
Than one's range of expression, so that photographed
It never looks twice the same, and people say
'But that's not you!'

One would like to reply:
'No, that's not me, because I'm incapable
Of starting the very least personality cult.
I have freed myself at last from being me;
Don't think of me as chameleon or actor; if I take
Protective colouring, it is that I mean to be
A kind of medium, free to enjoy, well, *no identity*.'

FIVE WILD ORCHIDS

I hunted curious flowers in rapture and muttered thoughts
in their praise – John Clare

We won't pick nor let a camera see
these perfect five,
nor tell a single person where they are.

I see their tint and detailed singularity
delineated by a fine, devoted hand
some sunlit sheep-bell afternoon, two centuries ago.

Next year they may increase
or not, along this untouched slope in June,
this unfrequented mild escarpment.

Unlikely we'll be here again
to see the silk-
winged inflorescence on new stems.

We've interrupted their rarity.
With rapture, with praise, with deference
we back away, muttering.

THEY

Do you think about them at all? They
either don't think at all, or think nothing,
or think vaguely of you. They
think what's good to be done or is done well
is only so if done by their own set.

You've been and have done what you could
by being yourself, not one of a set. They
in their zipped-up self-importance
hear your name (they do just hear your name)
condescendingly. Some even praise you.

You once made the mistake you could only
make once, of being young; and so provoked
in them (as they then were) some envy.
Life's motor is habit, so they went on
calling you young till you were bent like a boomerang.

They've stayed unchanged while the usual process
was cutting deep glyphs in your withering face,
but when your hair turned white in a single
decade, they saw it was high time
to disregard you and write you off as stale buns.

As you have for some time built up
what you could against the ravening ebb-tide
with what skill you had and as chance allowed,
and since what you built has form
and is still added to, it's not unknown. They

seeing it not unknown can't quite ignore it. Now,
if they praise, they praise you for what
you're not, or for what they allege you
to have once been. With quaint smugness
they applaud their false image of you.

Oddly supposing some judgment needed from them
yet always flummoxed by the imaginative,
or prophetic, or creatively marginal,
they compare it to what they fall for –
the trivial, the trendy, the ephemeral.

If you happen to waffle on to a great age
they'll allow you a slight curiosity-value
as a survival of a species almost extinct;
they'll patronize you with a show of false esteem,
unaware that you seldom read or hear what they say.

It's plain that by deviating in your own way
you've made what you have. You've made it
clear, durable, pointed as a cluster of crystals. They,
they have grown nothing but a great goitre
of mediocrity – not only unsightly, it's incurable.

PASSED BY THE CENSOR

*The Publications Control
Board has decided to allow
South Africans to put ice-
cubes made in the shape of
female nude dolls into their
drinks. Disclosing this infor-
mation at a women's gather-
ing this week, a member of
the Board, Mrs J. P. Theron,
said it had been decided to
allow the dolly ice-cubes
because they melted so
quickly in the liquor.*

> *The Board was not nar-
row minded, said Mrs
Theron — Cape Times*

What a corrupting new device!
But in this case my ruling is
   Our rules need not be rigid:
These topless girls are bottomless,
And though they give one melting looks
   They're pure. What's more, they're frigid.

WHITE GLOVES

Reading some Russian novel
    far on a Transvaal steppe,
blue hills near in the clean sky's lens
    and Russia brought quite as near
in the focus of prose, the place I was in
    and was not were strangely merged.

Straight as a caryatid
    a brown girl held on her head
a brown girl's burden of white things washed
    for whites, of whom I was one:
she knew she was graceful, I knew
    her life was the life of a serf.

Now, with half a century gone,
    a letter that comes from those parts
shows by its turn and tone of phrase
    it comes from a Tolstoi-time,
from a sun-dried Russia where even now
    the serfs have not yet been freed.

A terrace in lilied shade,
    ice clinks in glasses there,
white gloves disguise black hands that offer
    a tray – untouchable hands.
Can race to a feast. On the burning veld
    slow peasants stand apart.

The scene dissolves to Kazan:
    the snowy versts race past,
wrapped snug in furs we chatter in French

as with clinking harness-bells
we drive to a feast. On the frozen road
   slow peasants step aside.

Some other caryatid
   no doubt, after all these years,
barefoot and slow, with patient steps
   in the place I knew upholds
with her strength what has to be done:
   the serfs are not yet freed.

Not of them the letter brings news
   but of a picnic, a bride,
white bride of the son of a millionaire,
   and of pleasures bought. It implies
that a usual social round
   runs on its inbuilt power,

runs by itself, by right;
   will last; must drive, not walk.
Alone and apart, more alone and apart
   it floats, floats high, that world
with the tinted oiliness
   of a bubble's tensile skin:

but inside the bubble a serf,
   black serf, peels off his gloves,
white gloves. With naked hands
   he opens a door FOR WHITES ALONE
and salutes in a mirror the self
   he is destined at last to meet.

DEATH OF A HEDGE-SPARROW

This afternoon it stood alone,
Beside me, showed no fear,
Resting its head between its wings.
After an hour it moved, it fell,
Under a tower of leaves
Careened, and there it lay.

There as it lay, its thin,
Its thorn-fine claws
Encircled emptiness;
Its dew-bright eyes began
To blur. Its pin-point beak
Drank three quick sips of air.
Then it half seemed to sigh,
Stretched with (too faint to hear)
One last, fan-opening whirr
To full extent both wings,
In flight from life;
They slowly closed.
It shivered once; lay still.

To mind there sprang
A Roman phrase, *Ubi humilitas,*
Ibi majestas. Great marble word
For an almost weightless corpse!
My little pang was not excess
Of sentiment, it was proportionate
(Sole witness, I affirm) to what I saw.

NOW

I

Lonely old woman, her husband died
on some useless alp.
Lonely old woman, widow
of a lost civilization.

A prisoner of habit, at home
she has lived on and on, inside a dream
of her safe early years
in a lost civilization.

This once quiet by-road's now a by-pass.
Her well-built house stands well back
half hidden by trees,
and not yet for sale.

'Rare opportunity,'
some agent will announce,
'gracious detached
character residence of older type,
might suit institution, requires
some modernization,'
having been planned for
a lost civilization.

Prodding and peeping in this acre of jungle,
once a garden, a modernizer
may break his leg, snared
by a rusty croquet-hoop
or the lead rim of a half buried

ornamental cistern.
There's no gardener now.

Like the house its owners
were gracious, detached,
thought it wiser not to love
one's neighbour as oneself,
wisest
to be only upon nodding terms.

As clear as an inscription
their thoughts could be read:

> Presuming on propinquity
> neighbours might show themselves,
> might show curiosity,
> or, by asking questions,
> familiarity.

> How appalling
> if they were to speak
> about themselves!
> They might try and impress one,
> or, absurdly, pretend
> one couldn't impress them —
> as if one would ever bother
> to make the attempt!

> I suppose if appealed to
> in some crisis
> one might be driven,
> yes, driven by imprudence,
> to play the Samaritan.

II

Under the heavier and heavier alluvium of noise
deafness has silted up and sealed the house.
If unremembered, as if Etruscan, painted rooms
rare and hand-made undiscovered things are waiting,
finely made to last, things handed down
and kept with the respectful care of those
accustomed to good things – things touched and seen
almost as if animate, things heartfelt.

To have assets or have food to eat
was once inseparable from thanks; wastefulness
by rich or poor, so it was taught,
was wrong; but avarice was despised.
Now by-pass lives are caught up in a complex
of invented needs that money-suckers boost
for quantities of trash, fallible,
expendable, much of it indestructible.

First thing in the morning, drawing back
threadbare curtains to light her loveless days,
habit makes her note the night's additions
to the day's, to every day's, disjections:
over her straggled hedge bottles and cartons fly,
cans, another broken mattress, one more white
up-ended broken stove, and nameless things,
conglomerating a malignant growth.

III

'Horner has died, who used to put things right
and keep things straight for me, and keep things clean,
and make things grow. He fought for tidiness
against the weather, gales, weeds, pests.

121

"Mustn't let Nature have her way," he said.
He knew that gardening is an art. I used to think
he seemed in the garden like a worshipper,
bowed down and kneeling all those devoted years.

'Now Mrs Horner's gone. Twice the corner wall
of Mrs Horner's cottage quite collapsed
under the impact of a ten-wheeled lorry.
Neither time was Mrs Horner, who did everything
for me, there in the room. So fortunate!
"It would be tempting Providence," she said,
"to use that room again." After repairs
she always kept it locked, and empty too.

'In this house now I only use two rooms.
Thanks to my deafness, I don't hear them now,
those dreadful lorries, like warehouses going by,
and motor-bicycles, so fast, the wild young men
fly past with streaming hanks of hair
jerking back in the wind like snakes,
and frantic fringes on their leather coats –
off to their coven, I fancy, on some blasted heath.'

IV
'As for me, I never mope.
I dodge self-pity like the plague.
Hope? A drug I'm now immune to.
I expect to finish here, alone.
If I collapse, am found, and driven away,
what good would that do? None.

'I'm light as a feather now,
dry papery skin, and like my mother
I'm small-boned.
I can imagine after a long delay
forcible entry, and what was me on the floor
like a discarded summer travelling-coat,

'or like a dried-up butterfly
(butterflies never learn that the finest fidgeting
continued and continued even all summer long
can never make that wall of solid air,
a sheet of glass, a sudden
change to freedom),

'or like the sloughed skin of a snake
(I hope I may say non-poisonous).
Lying there, I'll be proved less durable
than my Tudor spoon, my Hilliard,
or my melon-slice of jade.
Exquisite, isn't it?

'One hope I have, that these few pretty things
inherited or acquired, outlasting me,
may be cherished for what they are
more than for what they'd fetch.
Who, you may ask, is to inherit them?
Leaving the world, I leave them to the world.'

123

FORMER MIGRANTS

Outdoors, in metal canisters on wheels,
Indoors, all gaping at a box of tricks,
How might we seem to former migrants here?
Addicts of felony and trash smeared thin,
Drugged by the instant, with collapsed
Imaginations, passive, levelled down.

By Blake, along this now unlikely coast,
'Celestial voices' were 'distinctly heard';
Hudson, lone exile from the Purple Land,
'Wrote as the grass grows'; Jefferies, true
Life-loving countryman, was downed by pain;
And Wilde, in this unconscious town, displayed
The importance of being frivolous and rash:
Beyond the aerials, these perpetual stars.

AFTER THE PERFORMANCE OF
A NŌ PLAY IN LONDON*

Out from that archaic art
into a street at night
all is unreal,
torn headlines slurred,
tyres racing off
towards what?
All is unreal except
that stylized myth,
vibrant bronze bell-tongue
in the urban blur,
clear as a new green
sunlit bough of leaves
hung by reflection in
a deep black pool;
so transmutation
startles and elates.

* From a notebook of unpublished draft poems.

A RADIO INTERVIEW

In memory of Cecil Day-Lewis

'When young,' he was told,
'I seem to think, and wouldn't you say,
You turned your back on the old,
Then got swinging into your stride
In your own way?'

When the dying poet replied
His voice went faltering firmly back
With difficult steps, difficult steps,
Over his former training-track
To recall the pace he could never regain.

'And what,' he was asked,
'Of those menacing years, that terrible phase,
With the Hitler thing, and the war in Spain?
Did you still feel hope?' One single phrase
In his answer rang with emphasis:
He clenched the words 'I was full of hope!'

Incredulous at hearing this,
'How could he?' a listening friend cried out
(Not an especial misanthrope
But his youthful veins had been drugged with doubt
And frustratedness, as if injected.)

'How little I knew him! I supposed dismay
Universal then, and the very air
We breathed infected
With anxiety, apathy, despair.

'Unravelling all day
My ignorance, I understood
Hope of a sort myself had lacked,
Gathered perhaps with the stored and stacked
Harvest of early fatherhood.

'Myself had been several ways displaced,
Putting out premature flowers in haste
As shallow transplants do;
Slow the renewal of a broken root,
Slow, slow before I grew
Soundly, and set some fruit.

'Hope in me was long asleep
Though awake in dreams. I couldn't accept
Utopian reckonings. Even now I keep
To a private path, as then I kept –
But when mine crossed his, a pleasure!'

Children of a horse-drawn day
In a high-speed world, at our leisure
We felt, as coevals may,
Compatible in a brotherly way.

PAINTED ON DARKNESS

A sunlit branch of four reflected roses
Bright on the darkened window of that room,
That locked and shuttered, memory-haunted room,
Startles by tint and stillness, perfectly composed.

Each rose transmuted, sweeter than itself,
In pure vermilion stands out strange and new
Against the haunted glass intensified,
Painted on darkness, as a poem is.